Confessions of a Cheerful Giver

Judy Madsen Johnson

Confessions of a Cheerful Giver

Copyright © 2018 Judy Madsen Johnson

ISBN: 978-1-945975-69-1

Published by EA Books Publishing a division of
Living Parables of Central Florida, Inc. a 501c3
EABooksPublishing.com

DEDICATION

Dedicated to the memory of Mary C. Crowley

Founder and President of

Home Interiors & Gifts, Inc.

Mary's reliance on the Holy Bible and the attributes

of an all powerful God

Impacted and inspired others to strive for their full

potential

To His everlasting glory!

PROLOGUE

"Teach those who are rich in this world not to be proud and not to trust in their money which is so unreliable. Their trust should be in God, who richly gives us all we need for our enjoyment. Tell them to use their money to do good. They should be rich in good works and generous to those in need, always being ready to share with others. By doing this they will be storing up their treasure as a good foundation for the future so that they may experience true life" I Timothy 6:17- 19, (NLT).

Chapter One

Jerry Lewis, the comic actor and producer of Muscular Dystrophy telethons, used to tell his television audiences, "Don't give until it hurts. Give until it feels good." Obviously, the sacrifices he made to raise millions of dollars felt good to him. Imagine how it felt to those men, women, and children whose lives were improved. This principle, often overlooked even by Christians, was one I learned early-on to embrace.

As a young couple, my husband's commissions provided our household income. There was no way to anticipate the size of our paycheck, so I prayed for our debts to be wiped out. In this situation, tithing was not seriously considered. It seemed a contradiction to consider tithing if we were just scraping by. However, my journey toward a generous life would involve changing my attitude about giving to the Lord.

Even yet, giving small gifts brought satisfaction as I learned the truth, "it's more blessed to give than to receive." I couldn't let the offering plate pass by without putting something in, even if it was very little, but it was something of an afterthought.

Gilja would change that. Two-year-old Gilja, like many other survivors of the so-called "Korean Conflict" in the '50s was left an orphan. Our adult Sunday school class "adopted" her, not in the legal sense but as a spiritual commitment to demonstrate that Christians in faraway America loved her. In our midst, we had already experienced the joy of Korean babies with glossy black hair framing smiling chubby faces. Several Park Lake Presbyterian Church couples had adopted these special gifts from Asia.

Monthly donations were sent to the orphanage in Seoul where Gilja lived. When she turned five, we took turns writing her letters and sent wrapped presents at Christmas and her birthday. As she learned to read and write, we received her happy notes with colorful art. My husband and I gave $5 a month — this small mite gave us much cheer. In return, we were learning, like Jerry, how good it felt to give. Perhaps putting a face to the gift had changed our perspective.

They say when one is confronted with a life-altering crisis, the response is often to take an inventory. I did that and pondered why my spiritual growth had been so slow. Why did I eat Pabulum for so long instead of savoring the meat? Why had I not learned to exercise my faith from the beginning?

I knew many religious platitudes, but practical day-to-day application of the tenets of Christianity had not become the air I breathed. But when I finally laid open my soul's quest to honor my heavenly Father, I found the answers I had long sought. This book reveals my journey.

Confessions of a Cheerful Giver

Chapter Two

When I was a child, I would have said we were a Christian family, but that is not true. Ours was a moral, hard working, lower middle-income class family. I think the same was true for my mother growing up in her grandparents' home. Most likely Episcopalian, but Christian? I don't think so.

My father, however, was a choir boy, singing with other boys to the organ music his father played. When he left England and immigrated to Canada, it was a Church of England priest who made arrangements for him to have a job waiting and a place to live.

But the only times I remembered being in church as a small girl was on Easter Sunday morning, at my younger brother Dickey's christening, and various family funerals. So I never experienced being taken to Sunday school or church services during my early childhood years. The one exception was Vacation Bible School at a Lutheran Church in Dayton where I enjoyed doing crafts and hearing Bible stories for the first time.

We moved to a small southern Ohio town the summer before I began the fourth grade. In Seaman, my best friend, Juanita Steen, and her family invited me to go with them to the Mt. Leigh Presbyterian Church. I joined the church within the year.

In 1944, I received my first Bible — a beautiful, gilt-edged, black leather, King James edition with red-letter quotations of Jesus. The day I received this unexpected Christmas gift from my parents, I leafed through every thin page, feeling so blessed.

Surprised by Mom and Dad and this wonderful present, I began to think that perhaps they were pleased with my becoming a Christian. More than likely, the seven-day weeks my dad worked precluded any time to spend with the Lord — as he gave his best efforts to support our family. He confused me though, as I heard him say when religion was discussed, "I don't wear my religion on my sleeve." Many years later, he openly shared his faith.

I wanted the story to be different when I had children of my own. We would be a family going to church together, making spiritual memories, growing in faith and maturity. My husband, Bill, had a Christian family who had always worshipped together. That bode well for raising our children in a godly way.

Learning to share, putting others first began my children's early lessons in giving. I wanted to provide them many creative ideas to give useful gifts and leave a part of themselves with others.

When I taught four-year olds, we took the class, including our kids, to a home for *exceptional* children, bringing pets, treats, and homemade cards. How these kids thrilled to pet or touch animals, which were beyond their realm to own. Exposing our children to others with severe handicaps gave us opportunities later to discuss our blessings— being healthy and able to run and play and go to school. When asked to pray for these whom God also loves, they readily bowed their heads and folded their hands.

The next Christmas season, Bill brought along a keyboard from his music store when we visited senior citizens at their nursing home. We sang carols and presented them with homemade goodies. Small gifts, but ones that brought much cheer. As we hugged each resident goodbye, their radiant smiles touched our hearts. In that moment, Jesus was near.

We never missed attending church on Sunday mornings, but mid-week prayer meetings didn't fit into our family work schedule. After years, our church dispensed with them because of scant attendance. Eventually, Sunday evening services in the sanctuary also disappeared, except for the active youth programs, which had meant so much to me through high school. Thank God, they are still a mainstay for young boys and girls, vital to their development with a balanced mix of spiritual instruction and wholesome, fun times. Youth leaders are a special breed of people.

Chapter Three

At fifteen I signed up for summer church camp. My Presbyterian minister didn't have to twist my arm, but I wondered why no one else was going. My parents drove me to Danville, KY, the Centre College town. It hadn't really bothered me that I didn't have some chums with me—I made friends easily, a byproduct of my dad moving our family around a lot. The first night's icebreakers did the trick, practically every minute something was popping, and my roommate turned out to be really neat. Camp was off to a great start.

We had daily assembly with speakers. Sports and competitions appealed to my athletic interests. Meals were filling, but nothing to rave about. What I liked best was the evening vespers at sundown when we found a solitary spot to call our own on the green. We sat with our Bibles and suggested readings. We read or prayed, or both.

Music wasn't so popular as it is today with youth. Without television and teenage celebrities, few were involved musically, except in school choruses or band. But we knew the hymns from the standard hymnal and sang them enthusiastically.

The First Presbyterian Church of Danville, a beautiful Gothic-style church with stained-glass windows, stood on a corner of the college campus. On Wednesday evening we gathered in the sanctuary for a worship service.

A young pastor gave the evening message. I heard every word clearly — it seemed he was speaking right to me. It was a salvation message, and I hadn't been exposed to the gospel in just that way. I'd never heard an altar call before, but a strange stirring of my heart compelled me to walk down the aisle to the altar where the pastor stood. A few others rose from their seats ahead of me. When I stood before the pastor, I felt that I was alone in a moment divinely set apart.

Whether the church had a cross or not, I can't remember. But ever so strongly, I envisioned that I was standing at the foot of Jesus' cross. My head bowed, I heard the words, "Beneath the Cross of Jesus" being sung quietly:

> "Upon that cross of Jesus, mine eye at times can see the very dying form of One Who suffered there for me; and from my smitten heart with tears two wonders I confess— The wonders of redeeming love and my unworthiness"

Drop by drop—on my head, my shoulders, and my feet—I experienced *blood from Jesus' pierced side* falling on me. I cried with a broken and contrite heart. I knew then that I had caused His death and asked Jesus to forgive my sins. The pastor prayed with me.

Then, the pastor gave me bread (the body of Christ) and grape juice was passed (the blood of Christ shed for me). I had communion before, but never like this. I knew I'd been *born again*. I returned to my pew, cleansed and free.

Back at the First Presbyterian Church in Somerset, KY, no one asked me anything specific about camp. I wanted to tell my minister, but held back. I never heard the words, "born again" mentioned in our church, like it may have been too fundamental, not *religious* enough. I suppressed the joy I had felt at camp.

Literature began arriving in the mail. Probably because at camp I had filled out a card or signed something. "This is the year of *The Call*, and we need leaders." The material came and I shrank back from following through—it was my secret, my shameful secret.

Was I supposed to become a missionary now? It always seemed to be Africa that was the subject of missions, and at the time, the Dark Continent everyone wanted to avoid. How could I leave my home and go to Africa? It all seemed so scary. These private thoughts haunted me.

Never had I heard a missionary speak, and I was in my mid-teens. I never knew of anyone who had gone to the mission field. *Where did they come from? Wasn't I supposed to be different now? Had I failed God so early in my weeks of knowing Him?*

In the intervening years between my teen and adult life as a young mother, I was no closer to meeting a real missionary. My conscience relaxed after convincing myself I was not called to be a missionary. Even so, my questions were left unanswered, and yet I remained quietly fascinated about this elusive mystery.

Our denomination's support for missionaries seemed impersonal. The emphasis came just once a year, allotted from the church's budget. We didn't receive regular notices that real people—each with a different story— were isolated from everything that was familiar in their lives. Every three years or more, missionaries came home to rest and refuel—at the time we called these returns *furloughs*. And just like our forces in the military, I'm sure they had many battles to wage. We never knew the extent of their personal sacrifices.

So few of the congregational family would come to hear these precious people, strangers to many of us, unless it was during an already scheduled service. As I began to sort all this out—that we, as a body, fell short of God's standard—my life took an enormous hit.

Chapter Four

Our third child had been born two years before; our dream home constructed that same year. It seemed our life was on an upward trajectory, and maybe brighter days were ahead. But, there were barely perceptible signs that it might be otherwise. Almost ten years into our marriage, my husband left us. Left me.

There was never any explanation that made sense to me—other than he didn't love me anymore. It seemed unfathomable that two people who had matched up so perfectly before marriage had arrived at this place. After two and a half years of separation, a divorce tore our family in two, permanently. *This doesn't happen in Christian marriages.* But it had in ours.

My new status caused stressful days and endless nights of muffled sobs into my pillow. Guilt accused me of failing my children. They had to be hurting as much as I. They probably tried to answer their friends' awkward questions, but wondered themselves if they were part of the reason Daddy left.

Attending church remained our default position, though I felt embarrassed every time I entered the church. In spite of my self-pity, I remained in the Couples Sunday school class and drew closer to God. I had no other anchor, and His care over my children, either through guardian angels or people with skin, lifted my depression and set me solidly on the Rock.

> "The Lord is my strength and my shield; my heart trusteth in him, and I am helped: therefore my heart greatly rejoiceth; and with my song will I praise him" Psalm 28: 7, (KJV).

Years later, I would marvel at how well adjusted my kids had become. God was indeed faithful.

Chapter Five

Spiritually I landed in a better place, but it wasn't long before finances were stretched to the limit. As a stay-at-home mom, I needed to take up the slack by getting an outside job.

When I first started selling Home Interiors & Gifts Accessories (HI), my home still had bare walls. The company gave me a loan to buy my display case. Mary C. Crowley, the President of HI, had been a single mom before age 20, eking out a bare existence for herself and her two children. Perhaps I could copy her example of hard work, self-confidence, and belief in God. She embraced the Christian dynamic as a businesswoman and built a multimillion-dollar sales organization.

Mother balanced my checkbook, and I was spared worrying over whether I had enough to pay the next mortgage payment. My parents moved when

Firestone transferred Dad, and a friend volunteered to handle my bank account. Later, I learned that Toody Brush had sometimes covered my shortfalls until I had enough in my checkbook to pay her back. She never told me. God took care of me by these quiet acts of kindness.

As a single mom with three children to support, I learned what it was to struggle. I never sought welfare or free school lunches, and neither did we go without. I had learned much from my parents' Great Depression-style conservatism. For me that translated into: shop wisely, find the best bargains, and eat lots of Banquet chicken pies, Hamburger Helper, and Franco-American Spaghetti-O's.

Selling Home Interiors was fun, challenging, and fulfilling — even before I could say it was profitable — but I did feel rewarded by extra compensations. HI incentives included mink stoles, silver punch bowls, cups, and goblets, diamond rings and trips to Hawaii and Europe. I won each of these premiums over time.

Undoubtedly, the single best benefit I received from being a Home Interiors Displayer was recovery of my self-confidence. No job I had ever held before and during the early part of my marriage had given me so much satisfaction. I felt my customers' gratitude and acceptance. Handling these special accessories convinced me they were indeed the "jewels of the home." I knew there was more to gain from giving it my best for I saw how much other women had attained.

Chapter Six

The smartest move I ever made in HI was to share the business with my friend, Joyce Bright, six weeks after I signed up. She was my first recruit and we developed our decorating expertise together. In the beginning, we often brought to sales meetings the collaboration of our ideas and floral arrangements. Our friendship had never been so close. I had met her and Bill at Sunday school.

We both became branch managers, but it had been harder for her to qualify because she and Bill pulled up their roots in Merritt Island and moved to Atlanta. It was not easy for her to cold canvas for leads, but her hard work and perseverance paid off. She stayed with HI a few years longer than I, spreading HI business opportunities across Georgia.

Joyce, like myself, is a cheerful giver. She always showed her appreciation toward me for sharing HI.

Her displayers adored her. Well they should, because she expected great things of them, gave them goals and rewards to earn—topped by her inscrutable fairness and genuine love.

On her 20th anniversary in business, she ran a whopper of a contest—a Caribbean trip was the prize. Her displayers had to meet the requirements, but 'my' trip was an appreciation gift. What great fun we had—a large rollicking group, no doubt conspicuous by size and spirit.

It was either my third or fourth company seminar when Mom and Dad accompanied me on the trip to Dallas, happily expecting to see me receive rewards for goals attained. However, I set up a surprise for them. By prior arrangement, Don Carter, Vice President, came to my parents' table during the presentations and awarded them my European trip. My parents were speechless, and that didn't happen often.

My father was able to return to England, his homeland, and introduce Mom to his family. Their brother and cousin, Ted, was back with his American "bride" after leaving them at age 19. Several members, at odds with each other for *who knows what*, came together for the first time in years, and they were speaking with each other. What a good old time that must have been. There are no shy ones in the lot. My parents, the reconcilers, had the trip of their lives.

I owed my parents so much. They had provided me a happy, carefree childhood—not one with lots of material advantages, but a solid foundation of love, patience, and encouragement. While both gave me a sense of "You can do it, Judy," Dad was the super positive thinker. I got pushed into trying many different pursuits in school that were the source of a lot of belly laughs later. That doesn't mean I didn't get stage fright when standing in front of a large crowd, but it was all good training for what the future held.

Mother seemed to revel vicariously in my adventures. While she had done amazing things in her childhood, she hadn't had the freedom I'd been given. Once I'd outgrown certain mischievous capers, and spankings had come to an end, I got in step with my parents' program. Our happy relationship together helped me overcome a lot of the rough and tumble I later encountered as an adult. They deserved any additional happiness I could provide them.

Chapter Seven

However, five years into my decorating business, I still lagged behind as though treading water. I needed steady income and more of it. I desperately wanted something to grab hold of before going under.

Jesus said, "Come unto me, all ye that labor and are heavy laden, and I will give you rest" Matthew 11:28, (KJV).

Desperately, I needed that rest and reached out for the lifeline. Soon, I reached a plateau as Jesus began to reveal His plan in my life.

Mary Crowley built a gorgeous mountain top lodge near Buena Vista, CO in 1971, expressly for the purpose of holding manager retreats there. I was among the first senior managers invited, and eagerly anticipated my all-expense paid trip to Colorado.

Morning devotionals by Mary inspired me. She sat on a large hassock in front of the fireplace, her Bible opened in her lap. At our backs was the picture window with an unobstructed view of the strawberry pink mountain. Sunrises tinted the newly fallen snow.

One day, before breakfast, I went for a walk on the pinecone-studded trail. In the crisp air, I found a boulder to lean against while I counted my blessings. I reflected on the few hallowed days spent already in this veritable heaven on earth. *Why had I been chosen for this special privilege?*

Mary's devotional that morning told how she had put God first in her life, her family second, and her business third. I pretty much had it in a different order. But that morning I resolved to get my priorities straight, "make Jesus Chairman of the

Board" as Mary had done, and reorder the sequence.

First, I would commit to tithing. Second, I would fulfill my present responsibilities. They included a full Christmas season already booked solid with decorating shows squeezed into every available opening. Then, starting the New Year, I would limit my decorating shows. My goal was to spend more time with my children and focus on recruitment of new displayers. Stop spinning, as I had been doing, while trying to accomplish unrealistic feats.

Flying home, I resolved to persevere. The Lord tested me during the first few months following this goal. My income dropped, but I kept praying and redoubled my decision. By the end of the year, sales had quadrupled (new recruits factored into the increase).

Luke 6:38 came to pass before my eyes: "Give, and it shall be given unto you; good measure, pressed down, and shaken together, and running over, shall men give into your bosom. For with the same measure that ye mete withal it shall be measured to you again." (KJV) God had responded to my tithing of time, money, and service.

Chapter Eight

My trust in God had proven He is a Promise Keeper. I could, I WOULD, keep my promises to Him. Again in Matthew, chapter 21:22, He says, "And all things, whatsoever ye shall ask in prayer, believing, ye shall receive."

Mary Crowley first inspired my commitment, but Barbara Herrington, my girl *Monday through Friday*, more than anyone else helped me bring to fruition my plans and dreams. She had the organizational skills I lacked. Her common sense and hard work helped grow my business into a strong, thriving, moneymaking career. By the time she retired after 17 years of service, I had a portfolio worth over a million dollars.

In the beginning, however, I could only pay for part-time hours. Among all the wonderful ways the Lord accomplished His plan in my business, the gift of Barb as friend, confidant, and executive assistant was the best. Included in her many duties was keeping track of prizes, earned and awarded to my sales team, both from the company and also from my incentives to help them grow. As well as from the special goodies I earned as Florida Branch Manager.

Barb deserved bonuses as much as the rest of us, I reasoned. When I offered her a diamond ring or a trip to Europe, she didn't hesitate to choose a trip to the land of her ancestors. We enjoyed traveling together through France, Holland, Belgium, Germany, and Austria. My pastor was our director, and her upbeat personality endeared her to Asbury United Methodist members on the trip.

Often, there'd be uproarious laughter on the bus. Looking back to the source, there was Barb, the instigator, with her seatmate near tears from some joke or casual observation. Barb could have rivaled comedienne, Carol Burnett. She, plus my daily intake of German chocolate, made for a perfect day.

She received her diamond ring later. I purchased it for her in the Holy Land. No one could have been more appreciative than my Barb. I feel sorry for bosses who don't realize the value of faithful employees. My business training had focused on making everyone feel important. Those who give their best deserve a special prize from time to time.

"Hope deferred makes the heart sick, but a longing fulfilled is a tree of life" Proverbs 13:12, (NIV).

Chapter Nine

Back on track in my spiritual life, I wanted to build His Kingdom. My attitude toward missionaries warmed considerably when I met an older, but energetic couple, Russ and Rene Bothers. As Missionary Outreach leaders, the Bothers' emphasis and frequent contacts led us to accept missionaries as part of our church family. They had personalities, problems, and needs, and they were spread out across the globe.

One missionary in particular drew my interest, Marilyn Lazlow from Indiana. She wasn't a missionary to just one denomination. She was a ball of fire, a go-getter, and an energetic speaker. Her supporting churches dotted the U.S. map. A single woman, she was sent to New Guinea where there was an eight-and-a-half-hour trip by dugout canoe from Papua, the largest city to the remote jungle settlement with no written language. During her 17 years living with an indigenous tribe, former headhunters, she taught the men to read and write. She also translated the New Testament into their language.

The Bothers were planning a trip to visit Marilyn, and I had been asked to go along, but Rene fell and broke her hip. To my great disappointment, our postponed trip never rescheduled.

When Marilyn came back to the states, I drove alone to Zephyrhills Florida one evening to hear her speak in a small Christian Missionary Alliance Church. She presented her six-man team of translators in native dress, and told of misadventures in New York City. One of her team had decided to save his ice cream cone for later, and put it into his suitcase to take back to Guinea while others were saving their McDonald's hamburgers to show their friends.

Marilyn exuded enthusiasm and humor unlike any missionary I had heard previously. I felt privileged to give to her work. Since that time, I have found missionary outreach fascinating. I am encouraged by my present church's support for more than 20 different missionaries on five different continents. Not only are there summertime trips to give the youth a taste for missions, but adults may experience a short-term assignment to serve Christians elsewhere.

A church that *feeds the hungry, clothes the poor, visits the prisoners, helps the widows, and cares for the fatherless* is following His commands.

Chapter Ten

I began thinking about how I could honor the Lord and make a difference in another's life. I had always wanted four children and I was blessed with three. But what could a single mother, only recently established on solid footing, do about that?

Leaving a HI Manager's Convention in Dallas, I spent the weekend in Monterrey, Mexico. While on this brief R & R, the thought occurred to me to adopt a Mexican son. It seemed the streets were filled with small hustlers trying to make a few pesos, perhaps in need of a loving family. The American missionary next to me on the flight home provided a contact.

Much thought went into whether this was a pipe dream or the Lord's guidance. I shared with my son, Rick, that I wanted to bring another child into our family. He was only nine then, but we agreed a brother would complete our family. For two years, we set aside savings for a "Mexico or Bust" fund. When the time came, we packed our trunk with suitcases and two spare tires and set off in our Mercury Montego. My brood was 13, 11, and 8 years old.

Not all the boys at El Rancho del Rey were orphans. In fact, only two were eligible to be adopted. It's a very long story, but the happy conclusion to five years and thousands of dollars, five trips, and two attorneys: I wound up with two brothers, Pepe' the older child, and Raul.

That first trip, we felt forlorn leaving Pepe' behind at El Rancho—I would have to go back later after the legalities were satisfied. (Raul, the younger was nearly 13 when he came to the U.S., a few years later.)

We headed north toward Dallas. The wear and tear on our tires after a poorly thought-out side trip over a rugged mountain had slashed our tires, resulting in four flats.

Fortunately, I had my first Master Charge card, but I had brought it only to pay for gas, repairs, and rooms. Delays meant using up more of our food money. We were still south of the border when I called Lillian Banks at HI to see if an advance on my commission check could be cut and mailed special delivery to San Antonio to the Holiday Inn in San Antonio.

I didn't have a room reserved in San Antonio—it was just a hunch. I knew Hank Moller of Rancho del Rey had stayed there. Sure enough, the check sent by certified mail was waiting for us, but I couldn't get it cashed anywhere except at a bank, and banks were closed until the next morning.

All our clothes needed laundering, so we dropped them off at a Laundromat and headed to a Woolworth's lunch counter. I calculated the cost for our breakfasts and left all my pocket change for a tip. In other words, I hadn't a penny left.

So many of my trips in the past left me broke by the time my plane touched down in Orlando. I had much more reason to be confident this time around. I expected that my Abba Father would take care of me, and He always did. He has been my Jehovah Jireh, my Provider.

The bank required a Texas or military ID to cash the check of an outsider. After persuading the clerk to focus on the bank account of HI instead of the irrational rules required of me, he set off to have it approved by his manager.

A big smile flashed on his face as he opened his cash drawer, "You were right, it's covered. And then, he let it slip, "No problem, they have two million dollars cash in their account."

Chapter Eleven

My biological kids from the outset loved their new siblings and shared anything they had with them. My muchachos had the harder part—adjusting, assimilating, and chiefly, learning to speak English.

A special anecdote concerning our expanded family. I had some issues with one of the boys and needed a wise, male counselor. The Founder of Edgewood Ranch in Orlando provided the answers I needed. In friendship, he invited our family to join his community for their Christmas "Birthday Party for Jesus." My HI sales ladies helped me gather gifts for Edgewood Ranch's children. Our large boxful of goodies was brimming when my kids and I arrived for dinner.

The children of Edgewood Ranch treated us to a re-enactment of the nativity of Jesus, and after singing carols, began a procession of the youngest to the oldest bringing their gift to Baby Jesus. House parents had encouraged them to give Jesus something special. These children, so steeped in Bible stories, knew Him as their friend. Many gave their most prized possession, joyfully. Some gave the only toy they had. We witnessed true sacrificial giving.

Then Dr. Lynn turned around and presented these treasures to me to be sent to their Mexican counterparts, the boys of El Rancho del Rey.

You can't out give God! His surprises are the most amazing.

Chapter Twelve

When all my children but one had left the nest, I taught a college and career age class. During two Christmas holidays, we arranged to pick up shut-ins at a senior retirement community. We drove them to see a nearby living nativity scene, and toured beautifully decorated neighborhoods en route to my home. The lights sparkled in everyone's eyes. After serving refreshments, we returned them to Winter Park Towers. What a wonderful experience it was, bridging the generational gap.

One of the elderly ladies sent me a sweet thank-you after the holidays, and we became friends. For a couple of years we'd eat blueberry pancakes at I-Hop together, and I learned much about this stately spinster in her mid-nineties. I was truly enriched. God's curious irony—Westminster Winter Park, then known as Winter Park Towers, is where I now live!

My young adult children, their friends, and I sang Christmas carols annually in different neighborhoods. One year when the weather was inclement, we gathered at my home in front of a crackling fire, and dialed friends at random to bring them yuletide cheer.

"Hello _____, this is _____. We were headed to your house tonight to sing Christmas carols when a torrential rainstorm poured down. Now, we're gathered snugly at Mom's and decided we could carol you over the phone." (We sang three songs and ended each call with "We wish you a Merry Christmas.")

My kids have continued the practice, enjoying both good and bad weather, with their friends, children, and grandchildren. They've enhanced the tradition by hosting a supper beforehand in yearly rotation, and blessing the hosts' neighbors with their music.

"Joy to the world, the Lord has come, and heaven and nature sing!"

Chapter Thirteen

Mary Crowley brought a Para-church ministry, the Narramore Christian Foundation, NCF out of Pasadena, CA to my attention. Dr. Clyde Narramore, a Christian Psychologist, was a guest at our seminar. He and his wife, Ruth, debunked Freudian philosophy with solid biblical teaching. The couple traveled widely with their "One Day Personal Enrichment Seminars" and four-day retreats at conference centers across America before expanding internationally.

Their emphasis was on training leaders—lay people and professional counselors. As a HI Branch Manager, I felt it would be beneficial to expose my displayers, managers, and their husbands to the Personal Enrichment Seminar.

My sales people came from all over Florida to the First United Methodist Church in Winter Park. The

Narramores flew in from California. Ninety-five Madsen Branch sales people greeted them with great anticipation. I enjoyed a personal friendship with the Narramores after this introduction. That year, during the week between Christmas and New Year's Day, I took my family to Pasadena for a Narramore Bible conference and the Tournament of Roses Parade.

Visiting the floats the day before the parade was a fabulous experience. All of the materials on the surface of the themed floats were plants, leaves, blossoms, petals, and bark. The designers possessed great creativity; the floats were gorgeous and fragrant. It gave us a greater appreciation as we watched the parade the next day. In our rented car, we got to see a bit more of California, and enjoy the hills and valleys, the rugged shoreline, the perfect December climate. No stress, just a wonderful family vacation.

NCF included me in two of their tour groups. One, sailing down the Danube River, included a worship service in a Hungarian storefront church. We shared Christian literature behind the iron curtain, having taken it undetected through their customs inspection. The other, a Grecian tour led us up Mars Hill where St. Paul preached about the "unknown god." We took a cruise on the Aegean Sea to Patmos where St. John was exiled and wrote the book of Revelation.

Each February, the Narramores held a conference at the Lake Yale Baptist Conference center, where I heard common sense messages, and sang lots of old hymns. We were treated to trumpet, organ, and hand bell music by Ruth Narramore, and enjoyed fellowship with a variety of Christian folks, mostly from the north, including Mennonite believers.

An afternoon women's tea, a conference regular, drew the ladies together. Special treats and moving testimonies provided sweet fellowship. Dr.

Narramore would later smilingly tell the assembled group the most repeated story he heard, "Oh, we had a wonderful time, we laughed and we cried and cried." That, of course, constitutes the best ingredients for a ladies' meeting. The men should try it some time.

Clyde Narramore was a no-frills kind of guy; his wife, Ruth, the daughter of missionaries was born in China. It was always comfortable to be with them.

Later, when I jumped into the pro-life movement, I submitted my report about the experience to Ruth, the Editor of their ministry's magazine. The cover of "Psychology for Living" featured my photo of pro-lifers being arrested, and included the cover story in the centerfold. Not bad for publication of my first serious writing effort. I really appreciated their support and encouragement to save babies from abortion. Sadly, some Christians stepped back and treated the subject as though they would be contaminated by it.

Chapter Fourteen

Because of the Narramores, the value of Christian counseling impressed me greatly. When I met Dr. Hazel Goddard in Colorado, Founder and President of Christian Counseling Ministries (CCM) in the 80s, I was captivated by her down-to-earth style of helping people through their problems. Reading her book, "Can I Hope Again?" became a godsend, not only to me, but countless others.

After attending one of her fall conferences in Buena Vista, CO, I was hooked. This was my new annual conference, and every subsequent autumn, I traveled west when aspen leaves turned to gold. Asked to serve on her board of directors, I was impressed by the integrity and intelligence of the men and women who provided oversight. At the same time, I was flattered to have the privilege of serving with them. As years went by, Hazel frequently stayed at my home when in Florida. We became close friends.

More of my relationship with Hazel Goddard is featured in my book, "Fascinating Women, Living by Faith." Hazel had no peer that I was aware of in her chosen field of counseling troubled people. It was her style — personal, warm and friendly, yet still possessing the professional mindset — that made her stand out.

I sent several needy people west to work out their problems. Through Hazel's Chalet Retreat for Intensive Therapy, clients regained their equilibrium, sorting out damaging distractions, and returned home with new insights and coping mechanisms. How rewarding it was to witness their new outlooks, a result of their inner healing.

A second counseling office was opened in Daytona Beach, and I became the Board's liaison with her Florida counselor, Jim Coffield. Sometimes, Jim and I met over a buffet dinner in Deland to discuss ministry matters. CCM conferences were also held at the El Caribe Motel. During my years on CCM's board, I met many outstanding Christians. The connection I made with Jim led to later assisting him and his wife, Mona, in the adoption of their first son, Pearce.

After retiring from HI, I helped establish a Winter Park office for Shepherd Care's Christian Adoption. My vacant office became temporary headquarters until Marsha Goss, the new director, could settle into a suitable location. We organized an advisory council, and soon placement of newborns and hard-to-place children became our specialty.

Being present on the day of a placement thrilled me to the core. I offered a prayer and blessing for this special baby, and was rewarded with snuggles and rich memories.

Chapter Fifteen

It seems inconceivable now that I was treated to so many different areas of service, but the main, consistent element remained personal involvement — not just giving donations, but offering myself in the package.

My Sunday school teacher, Jim Gillian, invited me to a meeting of the Tom Skinner Club, an inner-city ministry in Orlando. I didn't know what I could contribute, but said "Yes." Unbeknownst to me, Jim was retiring from their board and offered me as his replacement. I met C. R. Smith, the founder of the ministry, a kind-hearted, compassionate man with an enormous heart for the black community. Who could refuse the privilege to help make a difference?

Many idle black youth had hung out around his furniture store. Driving his truck into their neighborhoods, C. R. and his gifted wife, Estelle, "tailgated" with the gospel. He preached and she taught the Bible lessons. C. R. was determined to keep the boys out of trouble and jail time. His tough love—the genuine kind—met a real need. Law enforcement agencies acknowledged his influence in reducing crime in Orlando where there had been gangs before.

I wrote fund-raising letters and helped rename the ministry—Frontline Outreach Ministry. Of the different agencies Frontline organized, a crisis pregnancy center taught abstinence and gave parenting classes. It was my early exposure to the evil of abortion.

Chapter Sixteen

During the years I served Frontline Outreach, I made two trips to New York City during Thanksgiving week to participate in "brainstorming sessions" between inner-city organizations, both in the Big Apple and scattered along the east coast and the South. The Smiths, another board member and I hoped to pick up strategies that would work in our ministry. There were plenty of successful role models to copy.

Rev. Paul Moore, a Nazarene and pastor of the Lamb's Church, was an innovator. He initiated Citihope, a radio ministry in the heart of Manhattan. He and his wife visited Orlando to help us implement ministry initiatives. I asked them to stay at my home.

Two serendipitous outcomes: They met my friend Gwyn Marolis who figured significantly in my life (she is one of the amazing ladies I featured in my book, "Fascinating Women, Living by Faith"). They recruited her to run their office in a skyscraper with a great view of the Statue of Liberty before relocating their ministry to a lower rent district in Andes, Upper State New York.

I also introduced them to Billie and Dana Edmondson of My Father's Love, a ministry serving disadvantaged and homeless people, and needy families living within their neighborhood. Paul Moore obtained funding for My Father's Love's small storefront outreach. The quarterly gifts lasted two years, a necessary boost at a time when the Edmondsons had been struggling.

Chapter Seventeen

Sometimes televangelists preach about giving to get back. Giving to receive was not something I carried over in my spiritual life, but it was a hard and fast principle in business. Giving in both spheres was evident in everything HI did. Mary Crowley was the most giving person I ever knew, and we women who worked for her respected and believed in everything she did or said or required of us. Mary always backed it up in daily practice.

Someone had given Mary two silver charms, which she wore around her neck on a chain. Whether Mary had used the insightful quote before the gift or after, I cannot say. But she was a living reality; the words personified her practice of generosity:

"I shovel it out and God shovels it in, and He has a bigger shovel than I do."

I've also heard it said, "Success is spelled W-O-R-K."

Though Mary Crowley was wealthy and seemed to have everything money could buy, she kept giving, giving, giving. There was no doubt that she still worked hard. But she reminded her managers, "There's no way you could work hard enough to earn this much money," or "This is the best-paying hard work there is."

Nevertheless, money stayed in flux. As we received bonuses — prizes for our diligent performance — so we passed generosity along to those whom we served. Qualifying for the position of branch manager, I began to see how much higher the stakes were. Each new unit manager whom I promoted in my branch received a celebratory banquet. Done in gorgeous style — the food, flowers, tiaras, evening gowns, and award presentations were incentives that had inspired their growth. At the end of the evening, the bill for the tasty repast was discreetly given to me.

Had I known when I was paying off my $100 case of samples at five dollars a month that someday I would spend thousands of dollars to help a unit manager achieve her goal, I would have said, "That's crazy."

Then there were manager retreats, managers' meetings at my house, and displayer recruiting contests and weekend holidays. My two managers, Nancy Tillotson and Althea Darling, promoted to branch level, joined me in finding desirable locations, planning entertainment and shopping venues. We shared expenses. We'd arrive at the chosen hotel/resort and prepare the evening meal in a suite before our ladies arrived.

The weekends began informally with lots of laughter and glee, a talent show or silly skits. When the weekends concluded, we had bonded and a new promotion was announced. The financial outcome proved whether we'd astutely calculated our income with our outgo. Mostly, I'd say it was guesswork. Win or lose, it was fun. Morale would rise.

The annual Branch Rally occurred in the fall and was underwritten by HI, and Mary chose whom she'd send to encourage and motivate us to end a bang-up year. Of course, as the branch manager, responsibility for organizing and delegation of duties was on my shoulders with the help of my two assistants, Barb and Marilyn Flaig. The largest one I planned was before I promoted the two other branch managers. My sales force was at its peak — around 750.

Our formal dinner couldn't have been more sumptuous. I had never seen such an enormous chunk of beef in all my life! The steamship round looked like a hefty steer had lost about 100 pounds around its middle. This time when I signed the check, the home office would reimburse it. I studied the bill: Steamship round...$500. It took my breath away. I had traveled far from Hamburger Helper in my small kitchen to prime beef sliced by a chef in a tall white hat.

Confessions of a Cheerful Giver

Chapter Eighteen

Packing in so much at a Branch Rally required a lot of energy on the part of everyone involved. I knew my efficient office staff would exceed my expectations, but I worried I might overlook someone or be distracted while in a conversation between sessions. It took so little to hurt someone's feelings unknowingly, thoughtlessly. The main point of these kinds of meetings was to build up, not tear down.

A new recruit in my personal Madsen Unit, Pat Nowling, was the mother of nine children and her husband, the father of five more. She worked fulltime as a waitress and he was a department manager for a super market chain.

Joining Home Interiors & Gifts was a real life changer for her. She was very neat in her appearance, had her hair done at the beauty parlor weekly, and her nails manicured, but she didn't own a single dress, and our dress code prohibited slacks. She decided she didn't want to pass up this chance to be more "ladylike" and bought a couple of dresses.

Pat hadn't made a reservation for the Branch Rally—I knew it was because she didn't have the money. There was extra space in my king-sized bed, so I invited her to my room. The rally would give her a huge boost as she was just getting her business under way.

At ten that evening, there was still much activity going on in the meeting room—displays being set up for the following morning, and ladies with their heels kicked off, hanging out together for fun and relaxation. But I was tired and wanted to go to bed before the big day coming up.

Evidently, Pat had had a full day herself. She came to the room and saw my "Living Bible" on the nightstand. She wanted to ask me questions, and I wanted to say "Good Night." Soon, I realized I was ignoring an important opportunity to share His Word. Answering a few questions led me to suggest that we set up an appointment the next week to go further in our discussion.

I stopped by Pat's home on my way out of town on a business trip, taking a Bible with me. It was another of those divine appointments where the Holy Spirit had already arrived. Pat prayed the *sinner's prayer* and received the gift of salvation. Over the weeks ahead, she lunged forward in her plan to see her whole family come to Jesus Christ as Savior

With 14 children, it took a while, and her husband held out a bit longer, but she was determined. When she later announced that she and Chris (not his real name) were teaching a Bible Study together, my gratitude soared. I had simply been "forced" to share with her – the Holy Spirit had done the real work in her heart.

Chapter Nineteen

Don Carter, our Vice President, figured prominently in HI's annual conventions. One of his pet projects was raising money for the Fellowship of Christian Athletes, FCA. For several years I observed dozens of items being auctioned off. Many of these were suppliers' samples, given to HI with hopes the items would be added to our sales line. Everything sold at auction represented 100% profit for the beneficiary, in this case, FCA.

Finally, I had the nerve to join in the auction, seeing that a few items were in a lower cost range. But the item I made an opening bid on, a flag plaque, soon took off into the stratosphere. In actuality, its cost as a hostess gift would be $6, but worth about $18. Denise Gore, Branch Manager from Nashville, was my bidding opponent. I was sure whatever the ending bid was, she could afford it better than I. Our two branches started cheering and egging us on.

As the pace began to accelerate, I decided to jump off after shouting, "$2,000."

But then Mr. Carter said, "Going once, going twice, sold to Judy Madsen."

Gambler's remorse best describes how I felt. My stomach did a flip! *Gulp.*

This giving was going to hurt. After the auction, I sought Don Carter to admit my insolvency ($2,000 being due then and there.) He gave me a few months to have it deducted from my commission check. Mary C. had passed by and said, "That was a good move—look how it has boosted the spirit in your branches.

Before the next seminar, I had to come up with a solution. I thought the FCA was wonderful, but my bidding had to be on more solid ground, backed up with plenty of *moola.*

I had held decorating workshops at several of the unit meetings, and the girls were very positive. I made sketches, showed color slides of wall groupings, and produced quickie floral arrangements. The glossary of decorating terms expanded their show dialogue. Word reached the others, and they were all asking me to bring the workshop to their next branch meeting.

An idea clicked in my head and "Madsen Branch Decorating Handbook" was born. Sales of the book would be committed to bidding at the next convention's auction. I introduced the handbook just before we left for New Orleans. In conjunction with a contest—the Madsen Branch displayer who sold the most handbooks would receive the premium auction accessory from me.

A displayer who sold 125 books while the hotel experienced their computers being down during registration earned the elegant eight-candle sconce I bid on and won. Pam Keaton worked the lines and delivered handbooks, floor by floor. I don't even remember my winning bid because this time I was not panicked. I had more than enough cash to cover it.

Chapter Twenty

Not only did the book sales pay for the item, all continuing sales profits after the convention were donated to FCA, Central Florida. The books were hot! News traveled across the country, and we sold over 3,000 of the Madsen Branch Decorating Handbooks. Thank you, Lord.

Every New Year's Day, Orlando's Citrus Bowl has the best college football teams competing. The FCA always hosts an athletes' breakfast before the big game. I was invited, but I thought *why would I want to be one of the few women in a male-dominated room?* So, I declined.

My son, Rick, received an urgent phone call from a friend who was on FCA's committee, saying, "You'd better get your mother there. She's to receive one of our plaques."

Rick, of course, escorted me to the event, which featured a high profile coach. Naturally, he gave a rousing message for athletes about to be pummeled, tripped, and tackled on the football field on New Year's Day. This was, indeed, a different kind of venue for recognition than I'd had before, but I took delight in being honored.

The next FCA President was an old friend, Gene Teolis, retired from IBM. He and his wife, Dottie, were my friends at church. Now I had an even stronger attachment to this fine organization. In later years, Rick's children were very active in FCA — officers in its government and song leaders and musical accompanists.

When I retired, my conference table and chairs, custom made for my home office was donated to FCA's boardroom. God's economy never ceases to amaze me. Ask Him what you are to do with this thing or that, which is no longer useful to you. He has the perfect place for it.

Chapter Twenty-One

Jesus, present with God at Creation, put stars in the sky, gave us the sun and moon, separated the earth from the atmosphere, made man and woman, and made all that there is (my quickie version of the beginning). Jesus is active even today in His Creation — thoughts in our heads that could have no other origin than from the omnipotent mind of God. He gifts us with remarkably creative outcomes. Some of this rubbed off each time I met new challenges.

For example, Louise, my housekeeper, worked hard and loved the Lord. Her presence in my life was calming and mutually trusting. For 23 years she served my family and me well.

Like others who provide domestic help in the home, she took a bus to her different jobs. After years of traveling — transfers and unexpected delays — by mass transit, she wanted to save and buy a car. Supporting five children and a husband who often was without work, made chances of success seem slim. Still she put aside her spare, very spare cash.

I told her that when she learned to operate a car, earned her driver's license, and saved enough to make two insurance payments, I would buy her a car. Louise was a biblical neighbor in every sense of God's Word, and this would facilitate those church calls to sick and bereaved members, and meals to the needy. I knew my small investment would help build the Kingdom through Louise, and my heart was merry. She wore out that Buick fulfilling the Lord's work, and bought her second car herself. God prospered her cheerful giving.

My first Cadillac, a good used one, needed to be replaced. Traveling all over the state to hold my branch meetings, I had racked up lots of miles. I learned that C. R. and Estelle Smith, God's humble servants, needed another vehicle for use about town. They were ecstatic about my gift of the Cadillac. I delighted to see C. R. arrive at our board meetings in his *new* car instead of the old truck he'd begun the ministry with.

As a young man, fast cars were my father's only indulgence. He had once chauffeured roadsters for his wealthy employer. Now, living on his social security check and small Firestone pension, those days were memories, long past.

I honked the horn and parked in his driveway the late model Mercury Cougar we had both earlier admired. When I knocked on the screen door, he opened it and caught a glimpse of the shiny black auto. Dad thought I had just bought myself a new car. He looked like he might faint when I handed him the keys. The Cougar replaced his 14-year-old Toyota Corolla. It gave him a slice of his youth back.

My favorite car of all, my last purchase, a 2004 Mercury, had been gently worn. I fought the insurance company over totaling it after a fender bender. I won. The Mercury was rebuilt and looked new and ran as good as before the accident. I gave it to Michele Herzog to provide transportation to abortion centers where she saves babies, and I pray it will serve her special purposes as well as it had mine. Being a cheerful giver has brought me so much pleasure.

More astounding was the manner in which the Lord used me to buy a single-engine airplane for Rancho del Rey. Theirs had crashed, but the life of Hank Moller was spared with non-life threatening injuries. The Holy Spirit gave me the total figure I should offer Hank. Stepping out in faith, I phoned him (without any idea where the money would come from), and my offer of $30,000 was accepted.

The Lord also persuaded the owner of the aircraft Hank made a bid on, $22,000 under their asking price, to sell his plane to Rancho del Rey. There had, naturally, been resistance in the beginning, but Hank would not let it rest until the gentleman said "yes." Then I borrowed the $30,000. Before the 90-day note came due, my income tax refund in the exact same amount arrived in the mail, and I was very cheerful. The refund also covered the interest on the note. The question is why be surprised at miracles if you have prayed diligently for them? The element of wonder and surprise has never left me, but I don't take miracles for granted.

Chapter Twenty-Two

Janice Kamp, an HI colleague, won a diamond ring and wanted to sell it to donate the proceeds to her church's building fund. I didn't need the ring, but wanted to help her meet her commitment. I seem to recall I paid $2400 for it. Soon, I fancied using it for a strictly personal reason, and I bartered it as a down payment on a time-share, receiving $3200 credit. The salesman then purchased the ring from his manager to give to his mother.

As he confessed to me, "I've missed too many of her birthdays and Mother's Days, and hope this will make it up to her."

The timeshare remained empty my two weeks because I kept so busy in my career. That seemed like poor stewardship, so I switched gears and began blessing others with it.

During the years I owned the timeshare, I gifted three couples each with a one-week honeymoon to the place of their choice and shared it with the C. R. Smiths for a much needed vacation. The timeshare afforded me space and quiet to work on my first book, and Mother and I had a couple of trips to the beach to relax together before Alzheimer's disease took her from me.

The final exchange, before I sold it, provided safe haven for a mother of seven whose abusive husband had made serious threats. She and her children enjoyed the beach while arrangements were made to help them escape to Germany to be under her parents' protective care. The relief and appreciation on her face as she boarded the airplane, holding her toddler, convinced me once again, "it is more blessed to give than to receive."

Chapter Twenty-Three

Along the way I became involved with Campus Crusade for Christ (CCC, later renamed Cru). The first crusader I "adopted" attended one of my Home Interiors & Gifts sales meetings at a Holiday Inn. I had hoped to recruit her mother, Maria, but she did not join the business. Instead, her daughter, Tina Woodruff, offered me a chance to support her, thus meeting Cru's requirements.

That was about 45 years ago. I wrote monthly checks for many years. Her ministry has been committed to those who serve in the military. Our friendship has survived the decades; we're still in touch and remain prayer partners.

Bob, a single friend of my son-in-law, joined the Student Venture ministry of Cru, and I supported him several years after his marriage and birth of a couple of children. Another young family with

Student Venture became acquaintances of mine because of a Chinese family I had befriended. They were mentoring the daughter, Jia Jia. When they were raising financial support, I had no extra money, but a diamond ring, I had won through Home Interiors, was my one available resource at the time. As I shipped it to them, I prayed it could raise a worthy amount for their ministry.

Donating material possessions came in handy — they were like money in the bank. You frequently hear charities advertising on radio or TV nowadays for donations of cars, boats, and other large items, but I was tilling the soil long before.

Jia Jia was nine the Christmas her parents Yuheng and Cuihua Boa came to Florida under the auspices of an International Christian ministry. I signed up to receive a single woman, but was offered this precious family instead. Yuheng, the father, was a post-graduate student at Ohio University. He was one of the first Chinese scholars allowed abroad following the "Cultural Revolution."

They were my guests for a week, during which time they visited the area attractions with their group. That still left prime opportunities to get to know them well, take them to church with me on Christmas morning, and have them share dinner with twenty-four members of my family.

An interesting item, one of God's coincidences is that I sprained my ankle the day before their arrival, and was trying to manage on crutches. Their presence in my home proved more helpful to me than I could have anticipated. One of their "treats" was getting to decorate their first Christmas tree. I could only sit and enjoy their pleasure. They pitched in to help me whenever their plans allowed.

Yuheng would exhort me, "No, Mama Judy, let me do that."

Cuihua and her daughter were Christians; Yuheng was not a believer when they arrived, but on Christmas Eve afternoon, I shared the gospel with him, and he received Christ as his Savior. It was as though he had been waiting for that special appointment.

The next morning at Circle Community Church, the pastor offered an open microphone for any who had a Christmas memory they wanted to share. Yuheng practically sprinted to the front to share his good news. His experience of salvation was certainly an emotional one.

The months following their return to Athens, Ohio, many trials beset the new believer. Persecution from Chinese students at the university caused Yuheng to lose his assistant professor's position. When the semester was over, I brought the Bao Family back to live with me for the summer. Otherwise, their financial situation would have remained bleak. I enjoyed eating their cooking, and our relationship grew firmer. It was the fortuitous summer of the Tiananmen Square Massacre, and emotions ran high when the Baos saw faces of friends on television as they were arrested.

Eventually, Yuheng and Cuihua returned to China. Jia Jia who received her education at the Air Force Academy was teaching there when we had our last contact.

Our ties have been broken, but I'll find them in heaven in *the sweet by and by.*

Chapter Twenty-Four

God began opening new doors by bringing other foreigners to my corner of the world. Godfrey and Stella Igbokwe and their young son arrived in the States from Nigeria for their college education at the University of Central Florida. They struggled to exist on their student visas, which limited the work they could do. Jim Gillean was Godfrey's professor and invited the couple to visit our class. On several occasions, we were blessed to reach out to them when Jim informed us that they were hard-pressed.

When Stella became pregnant with her second child, there were complications. A love offering was taken one Sunday, and I found my checkbook empty. I explained to Carolyn Gillean that I would bring my offering the following week. However, I forgot, and the matter was not brought up again.

Months later, my income tax refund arrived. Just as I was about to write my tithe check to another ministry, the Igbokwes came to mind…the first time I had thought about them since the empty checkbook episode. Earlier, my check might have been for $50, but $500 was the amount "whispered" in my ear. Using a midwife was not going to work when a caesarian operation was necessary, and Godfrey didn't have the $500 deposit the surgeon required.

I knew nothing of this development.

The couple prayed earnestly for God to provide this money, due within the week. My cashier's check arrived in their mailbox on the same day it was needed. I had sent it anonymously. In my mind's eye, I visualized Godfrey's bright smile and "Praise you, Lord!"

Chapter Twenty-Five

Once more, I tagged on to the Narramore Foundation, and a husband-and-wife team was sent to my home to teach Bible studies. A diverse group of devoted Christian friends including the Smiths, Teolis's, and Igbokwes came every week to grow in their faith and understanding. I began to know more sweetly the testimony of the Igbokwe family. Stella's father, a pastor, had sent each son and son-in-law to America and provided them and their wives' college educations. One of Stella's brothers had become a professor at Florida State University.

Because of the privilege of becoming friends with those whose motherland was Nigeria, the unique opportunity presented itself to practice giving in a way that caused me to more heavily rely on the Holy Spirit. I became "Mama Judy," available for counsel, encouragement, and when needed, financial gifts.

Years have proven the many blessings cheerful givers receive—directly from the hand of God. The Igbokwe's suffered financially for many years; they suffered separation, hard work, and deprivation. Never did they complain—"God is good," was always their reply. They gave sacrificially, knowing that God is no one's debtor.

When I was raising money to attend the UN Conference in Beijing in 1995 as a pro-life advocate, I wouldn't have asked Stella to give, knowing they still had urgent needs. Instead, I asked for her prayers, but she believed in my cause, The True Majority, Women Speaking for Women. Stella sent me a $250 check to help with my expenses.

Subsequently, their four children all earned their post-graduate degrees, and Stella, hers in nursing. There have been other huge checks from the Igbokwes, sent to me as a conduit for the ministries I support, or just to bless me. I have never refused them the blessing that is assured for the pure-hearted giver. God has rewarded their faithfulness and patience. I love them as my own children.

As with the Bao and Igbokwe families, "Mama Judy" became my identity. So it was with those of other lands including Mexico and the Philippines. Later, young mothers of babies who had been scheduled for abortion would choose that precious name, and our relationship began.

I never felt more respected and loved than by those who affectionately adopted me.

Chapter Twenty-Six

An injunction against me and other pro-lifers led to a U.S. Supreme Court case bearing my name. When I planned my trip to Washington, D. C. to hear Liberty Counsel argue Madsen v Aware Women's Clinic, I had no inkling a new ministry would be born. Michele Herzog had thought it would be a great opportunity to use my platform to draw attention to post-abortive women and the suffering they experience in silence. The True Majority, Women Speaking for Women became a force for those women whose voice was unheard.

The Lord anointed this ministry, which lasted for only four years, but accomplished significant results. He came alongside us as we raised many thousands of dollars in limited periods of time to attend United Nations Conferences. When the Lord raises up a ministry, He underwrites it.

His Word gave us hope, "And my God will meet all your needs according to his glorious riches in Christ Jesus" Philippians 4:19, (RSV).

Christians believed our advocacy for the preborn babies needed to be heard where the liberal feminists had control—in the United Nation Conferences—and they gave generously.

I traveled to Beijing, Istanbul, and New York City while other representatives went to Cairo and Rome. The Lord gave us favor as many delegates, particularly those from Africa, listened to our arguments and were persuaded to stand fast against abortion. Our faithfulness to serve God under difficult circumstances (that included 40 hours of house arrest) encouraged pro-lifers to defeat the pro-death delegates when the vote was taken.

Chapter Twenty-Seven

The good Lord continued His watch over me in matters of my financial affairs. The closest I had come to investments had been through HI's Comptroller, Bill Hendrix, and he had performed a superb service for branch managers. However, making a plan for my future became imperative.

I decided to retire six months after Mary Crowley's death. Leaving behind HI, a great 21-year career with fantastic ladies and lovely products, was not an easy decision. But, I wanted to become more involved in ministry. Thankfully, I could follow whatever opportunities the Holy Spirit brought my way as a volunteer and not have to be caught up in the daily pursuit of earning a living. He had made that possible. However, the unknown would still necessitate my total trust in Jesus.

Each time I had received an unusually generous check, often unexpected, there was a place to invest it...the timing was always perfect. Who else could it be but the Holy Spirit? As a retiree, unexpected checks would not normally occur. Fixed income was the operative word—except that the Lord has had the last word on that.

The Birckheads, Kent a financial planner and Barbara, a HI displayer had both been widowed in their first marriages. He impressed me immediately as a man of impeccable integrity. When we met, our values were in total conformity, and he offered ideas to help me build security for the future. His judgment was consistently steady and the tax advantages he recommended were put to good use.

Under Kent's management, I was able to attain a goal I had secretly harbored in my heart. One year, I was able to contribute 50% of my income to the Kingdom.

Malachi 3:10: "Bring the whole tithe into the storehouse, that there may be food in my house. Test me in this," says the Lord Almighty, "and see if I will not throw open the floodgates of heaven and pour out so much blessing that you will not have room enough for it."

However, what I hadn't counted on in 1986 is that I would retire from Home Interiors only a year later, (perhaps I was testing the Lord Almighty). A more conservative approach might become necessary, as my income most certainly would be reduced. Again the Lord provided.

My HI stock, purchased for $600 ($100 shares @ $6 a share in 1972 — my first bank loan) supported me when I retired at age 51 until I could begin withdrawing from my profit sharing fund at age 59½. The increase of those stocks had been phenomenal. When the stocks were gone, the profit sharing kicked in.

Profit sharing had been a reward for those at the management level who became fully vested. HI — not a penny from the managers themselves — made all contributions into the fund. From then until the time I'm writing this, this blessed reward has constituted my primary support. The old adage, "Waste not, want not" has timeless wisdom, but wisdom from the Good Book, shared by St. Paul in Philippians is unmatched,

> "For I have learned to be content whatever the circumstances. I know what it is to be in need, and I know what it is to have plenty. I have learned the secret of being content in any and every situation, whether well fed or hungry, whether living in plenty or in want. I can do everything through him who gives me strength" Philippians 4:11-13, (NIV).

Chapter Twenty-Eight

To continue on my path of security through stewardship, I accepted an invitation from Arthur Ally in 1994 to become a limited partner in a new venture, the Timothy Plan. The original partners put up the money, each according to their ability, to develop funds for those who wanted to buy "non-violators."

For example, a screening process eliminates any funds that support alcohol, tobacco, abortion, homosexuality, pornography and gambling. Today, two tools in keeping investments pure are screenitcleanit.com and biblicalstewardship.org. However, they weren't available when Timothy Plan was starting up.

One of our first goals was to provide a fund where pastors of small churches could establish their own investment plan for retirement. Eventually, even those larger denominational institutions with pension plans realized that much of what was being invested for them was *dirty*. It was a test of whether they were willing to divest themselves of *dirty* funds that were earning them dividends.

Months before Timothy Plan managed my portfolio, I had a financial planner that decided to transfer some of my assets into an Asian fund. He recommended more diversity, more growth. I was absorbed in something else at the time, and put off studying what this move might mean.

Thirty days had passed when I suddenly *saw the light*. I couldn't invest in anything Chinese — for heaven's sake; they force women to abort their babies. Even though now a Chinese mother may have a second child, any additional pregnancies will be aborted. I was heartsick and contacted the financial planner. "I must get out of this fund now." And then I added, "You know how pro-life I am, why, why?" His lame reason was the quick growth of the fund, and "besides, this is only 10% of your investments."

He continued, "Let me explain, if you change now, since the 30-day grace period has passed, you will lose over $25,000."

I didn't hesitate. "Do it now," I answered. I should have been more diligent in the beginning. "That one-drop of ink in a glass of water has colored the whole glassful."

The Lord honored my decision, and the $25,000 was earned back in six months with a clean investment. I was more than grateful. I was cheerful. Thank you, Lord, for lessons learned.

We, the Timothy Partners, looked at our limited partnership investment as ministry, unsure of what potential there was to grow our money. For years, no dividends were paid. The trustees decided to reinvest so that we could build our family of funds. Meanwhile, favorable publicity and satisfied investors, through *word of mouth*, have shown Christians there is an alternative that opposes putting your money where it honors the devil.

Today, we look back, after attaining a billion dollars in assets, and know that God has honored our faith and commitment.

To be sure, there are "Christians" who offer wonderful "opportunities" to profit with their organization, but once I was caught in a scam that way. The entrepreneur, a former pastor, was *mining* his Sunday school class in one of the area's largest churches. When I heard about his *resume*, I also thought everything sounded solid. All of the investors were Christians whom I admired.

Later we learned that the monies invested with him weren't paying the mortgage payment on the property and he'd been using the money as a down payment on real estate in the islands. How he was going to pull this off we didn't know. I expect that his mysterious disappearance would have made headlines, but before that could happen, one of our partners suspected foul play and obtained a lawyer. I got back my one-time payment in full. The charlatan did time in jail, and the investors learned a valuable lesson. Perhaps, we were too eager to get rich.

It's clear that our Heavenly Father wants us to grow, either in wealth or talents. The Master's angry reaction to the man who buried the talent given him leaves no margin for doubt. But what is our motive? Is it to help others or elevate ourselves?

> "Do not store up for yourselves treasures on earth, where moth and rust destroy and where thieves break in and steal. But store up for yourselves treasures in heaven, where moth and rust do not destroy, and where thieves do not break in and steal. For where your treasure is, there your heart will be also" Matthew 6:19-21, (NIV).

Chapter Twenty-Nine

After retirement, I decided to look up my old friend, Joy Postle Blackstone, the artist.

Her studio had served a dual purpose, both a home and a place where she created her magnificent works of art. She had learned to live with minimum pleasures and conveniences for many years, but after fire destroyed her house on Lake Rose, a hot plate pretty much summed up her kitchen. Six-foot weeds on the lakefront practically obscured her water view.

My kids recruited a couple of friends, loaded up our old Chevrolet station wagon with mower, weed cutters, and a scythe, and we surprised Joy early one Saturday morning. By lunch, the ground had been cleared, and a canoe could again be launched as in past times when her husband was still alive. She and Pal, her faithful pooch, joined us on the porch as we shared lunches and chitchat. Our best gift to this aging widow was driving away her loneliness, adding to her joy. It felt so good to us—the kids couldn't stop chattering all the way home.

It was now 12 years later, and I found Joy at West Orange Manor, a nursing home in Winter Garden Florida. She had been bedridden for five years. Reunited, our friendship grew. I visited her weekly, unless a nurse called sooner and said, "Judy, can you come and get Joy, she needs a lift." I fastened her wheelchair in the van and we'd be off to parts known, often wherever water birds could be sighted. She'd be rejuvenated, rising again to ward off her circumstances.

She was once nicknamed the "Bird Lady," because of her Glamour Bird Shows, and it fit her well. I preferred to think she deserved the acknowledgment because her delicate renderings of her favorite creatures were unequaled. Or perhaps, I fancied, that somehow she was able to communicate with them.

Being with Joy was a gift I gave myself, but as her years shrunk into weeks and days, my presence and prayers also gave her peace as she finally rested in Jesus.

We wrote her life story together, and I believe that added a hope that she could be memorialized. It energized her until she couldn't fight the infection in her leg anymore. There's no way I could assess the mutual blessings God provided between the two of us. The final chapter of "Joy Cometh in the Morning" was typed the night before she died.

Chapter Thirty

My ministries lasted briefly in some instances, and with others, for many seasons. Sometimes I'd revisit organizations that have stood the test of time, offering new opportunities to engage. As my Cru connection had spanned several decades, I felt satisfaction when two of my dear friends, Gwyn and Kathleen, decided to answer their call.

Gwyn Marolis joined an associated inner city ministry, Citihope, in New York City. Cheerfully, I became her first donor. Eventually, she worked directly with Dr. Bill Bright, the Founder and President of Cru in Orlando. She served many years both locally as staff and in Paris as a volunteer. Gwyn had lived with me for a short time between reassignments.

Kathleen Martin was recruited for a year long commitment in Moscow, and I was pleased to help send her off to Russia as her first supporter. When she returned, she came to live with me and my mother, swapping hands-on care for Mom's Alzheimer's needs. My home was a "halfway house" for many. Halfway between assignments, folks in transition boarded though no money was exchanged.

> "Do not forget to entertain strangers, for by so doing some have unwittingly entertained angels" Hebrews 13:2, (NKJV).

My daughter-in-love, Wendy, took up residence with me on Lake Orlando Parkway shortly after she and my son Rick became engaged. Bringing her from her hometown to be closer to both Rick and me helped us bond in such a precious way. She has been like my daughter throughout their 32 years of marriage.

The Lord had provided me a lovely four-bedroom, two-and-a-half bath home with ministry opportunities on behalf of His servants. I was pleased when a couple who were on staff with the Brooklyn Tabernacle in New York City came for a few days of R & R. Likewise, Ralph Byrd, a counseling pastor, was served with a well-earned rest.

And though I was retired from HI by this time, I still enthusiastically extolled the benefits it had to offer to Ralph's wife, Valeria. It could be said that Valeria Byrd was my final recruit, and as one of the first recruits in Brooklyn, she invested herself in learning the business and became a big success.

Chapter Thirty-One

Pearl Burns was a Home Interiors colleague and dear friend of many years. After a long illness, her husband died, and she felt a deep void. I introduced Pearl to Cru, and she loved it immediately. We sat through a presentation of the *Jesus Film* ministry and she signed up for evangelistic trips utilizing the film. I signed up to underwrite the production of the film translated into the Nigerian Ibo dialect.

If I had thought Marilyn Lazlow was captivating, Paul Eshleman, Director of the JESUS Film Project and Vice President of Campus Crusade bound me in a spell. His book, "The Touch of Jesus" told stories of the risks and rewards of missionaries in the field with the film.

Joni Eareckson Tada had this to say in her foreword, "I always sit enthralled, listening to stories of modern-day missionaries taking the "JESUS" film to nations around the globe—hacking their way through thick jungles; over prison walls; down dusty, rutted roads; climbing treacherous mountains; and tiptoeing through dangerous political hot spots—all to show the love of Christ to a lost world."

I fantasized about how exciting it would be if I could join the Nigerian film team for their first evangelistic trip, carrying their equipment and film to the people in out-of-the-way places and wherever else authorities would let them pass. I wanted in!

II Corinthians 9: 7-8 says, "Each man should give what he has decided in his heart to give, not reluctantly or under compulsion, for God loves a cheerful giver. And God is able to make all grace abound to you, so that in all things at all times, having all that you need, you will abound in every good work" (NIV).

The $50,000 cost to produce the film was the last "miracle" gift I had to contribute.

When my check arrived from HI, I remembered that about ten years earlier, branch managers were invited to join a voluntary withdrawal program. Each chose the amount she wanted taken out of her monthly commission check. The company put the employee's contribution in a fund, a savings account. No one missed the withdrawal because it was automatic. I don't remember any account statement during those ten years.

When the company decided to end the program, checks were mailed to the participants. Some managers, like myself, had completely forgotten about the program, so it seemed like a miracle of the Lord's incredible abundance.

God timed it to arrive just before I attended the "Executives Retreat," a pilot program held at the Grand Cypress Hotel near Disney World. It was there I met Paul Eshelman. But, I was already well informed about the JESUS Film Project. I knew that millions had come to Christ when the gospel was presented to them in their own language.

Coinciding with the fall of Communism, production of the Ibo translation film was put on the back burner. Cru quickly seized the timing to counteract 70 years of atheism. They accelerated Russian translations in case their window of opportunity might suddenly close. This was a strategic move I agreed with.

Pearl made at least one of her evangelism trips to Russia before the Ibo project moved forward, and Paul Eshelman resumed writing me personal letters about the Nigerian translation's progress once it got underway.

I am sure we witnessed God's perfect timing. It was a few years later before the Ibo translation was completed and now millions have seen JESUS. Only God knows how many are now in heaven with him because of this project.

Chapter Thirty-Two

Pearl's trust in God's resources was not much different than my own. She, too, had made the most of her years in HI. She had been an outstanding leader, a Vice President when she retired. Her territory, the Eastern Area felt a great loss when Pearl left.

When Pearl married Jack Galpin, she and her new husband made trips to Siberia, Moscow, Macaw, and Nicaragua sharing the gospel with executives, educators, and military and political leaders. Then a fantastic surprise came my way.

She cheerfully treated me to a Jamaican trip. Others, along with Dr. and Mrs. Bright, were going to do street evangelism and share the *Jesus* film. I counted this a bonus, replacing the trip to Nigeria (and New Guinea) that had never materialized. Cheerful giving comes back to reward the giver.

In gorgeous Jamaica we were taken on a lovely tour, including a riverboat trip, stayed at a spacious resort, and enjoyed the tropical dining fare in sumptuous buffets. But we weren't there just to act like tourists. We had the privilege of hearing Dr. Bright's messages, and getting to know Vonette, his engaging wife. And there was more to come.

The JESUS Film project crew set up their outside screen and projector on the church grounds. Many people gathered on the lawn. Children tumbled and played until the lights went out and the film started rolling.

I had long ago seen JESUS in my own living room, but this was the spirit, the contagious excitement, I had long wanted to be a part of.

Many of the crowd professed to be Christians, but there were some young, tough, scoffers at the rear I had a chance to witness to, and brought Dr. Bright into their presence. I watched the bravado disappear, respect surface, and their attention captured as their leader allowed Dr. Bright to pray with him. I felt the Lord's presence. He won the day.

Chapter Thirty-Three

Through the Paul Moore connection I joined Citihope's ministry to go to the Republic of Belarus on a USAID mission. Our purpose was to distribute foodstuffs and medicines to people who had been struck hard in the aftermath of the Chernobyl Nuclear Reactor explosion. The catastrophe had occurred seven years earlier.

Belarusians had obtained their freedom from the former Soviet Union. Part of the goal set by Rev. Moore was to help them move from socialism to a democratic republic. The shipments coming over sea to Germany and over land through Poland to Minsk was enough to feed every man, woman, and child for two days.

These shipments of frozen food were distributed from warehouses contracted by USAID. The intention was to help privatize businesses —

breaking the communistic system, and give material aid to non-profit organizations.

My leaders had assigned me to Gomel, the city that sustained more illness and fatalities than anywhere else outside of the Ukraine. Acid rain had been carried by winds north and west, devastating populations, causing cancer and many other serious maladies. Some of the volunteers for our project, who arrived in Belarus, canceled, fearful for their own safety. I was given the choice to go or be reassigned elsewhere.

After praying about the situation, I was confident that the God of Israel, who had protected Daniel in the lion's den, and the three young Hebrews, Shadrach, Meshach, and Abednego from the fiery furnace, would keep me from harm. The devil may have had a win by those who folded, but my resolution to proceed resulted in my leading nine souls to their salvation. Is there anything that can give more cheer than that the lost are saved? It was more than worth the risk.

Confessions of a Cheerful Giver

Chapter Thirty-Four

A flier given me at church by a fellow member was an invitation to a pro-life rally the following Friday evening. During that week, I listened to Focus on the Family's radio broadcast. Dr. James Dobson interviewed Randall Terry, a young pastor from Binghamton, NY.

Terry had initiated a bold new pro-life movement, leading Christians to abortion centers where they put themselves in the way of abortion-minded women coming to abort their babies. Later, the statistics would show that 20% of the women who postponed their abortion appointments as "rescues" often necessitated, did not reschedule.

The pro-lifers were arrested, released on their own recognizance, and continued to repeat the process. Some, however, were not released. The charge: criminal trespass.

Thousands of Christians were responding to the call to "save the babies." Three days later, I experienced this call personally by a pastor, Rev. Ed Martin from Ocala. After deciding this was my duty, for the next 25 years, I *rescued* babies and their mothers from the tragedy of abortion. It had become my first priority. That even included, on several occasions, being arrested.

I directed financial gifts to pro-life work because many I considered heroes were losing pay, sitting in a cell, but still had families to support. No foundations or large 501c3's were underwriting their cause. One or two days a week, either alone or with a partner, I stood on a sidewalk calling out help to the mothers or offering to take the workers elsewhere to find another job. Outside an abortion clinic, a Christian message offers the last voice of reason. A final chance for a mother to change her mind. It seemed most of the world didn't care, but I was passionate — still am!

To say I was cheerful in this ministry would deny the many hours of disappointment when my pleas were ignored. But when out of the many who scorned the help, a single decision was reached to leave or go with me to a pregnancy help center; I could not have been more cheerful. It would make all the difference in the world to that one baby.

Had I still been advancing a career, I couldn't have been a spokesperson for the babies, a leader in the community and my church, rallying others to participate. Couldn't have become an influence in the lives of the mothers and their families, maintaining a relationship and spiritual motivation, as I have as "Mama Judy."

I couldn't have stood outside the centers and prayed and held signs. Couldn't have written letters and articles, and a book, "Stories from the Front Lines." I traveled to UN Conferences to fight the liberal forces pushing abortion on demand around the world because I could, and God was with me.

Chapter Thirty-Five

"It's not how much we give, but how much love we put into giving," Mother Theresa

God gives us opportunities all the time to be sensitive to those in need. City fathers have dispersed the homeless from certain spots downtown, but you see these unfortunate individuals most every time you're driving a car. Two of my experiences with them were not far apart. They both occurred on Saturday mornings after I left the abortion center.

I always fasted before my Saturday mornings on the sidewalk outside the abortion centers. Occasionally, I'd grab a quick breakfast on the fly before going home. Once, on a visit to a fast food restaurant, I carried a newspaper with me. I went inside, redeemed a coupon from the newspaper, and took a seat near the back. Directly across from my table was a gentleman intent on "housekeeping." He had a cup of coffee and six small creamers. He also had little cups with catsup and he'd capped them. After folding napkins, he placed them along with plastic spoons and forks into his pocket. God nudged me, and I asked the lone man if I could join him at his table. He seemed shy and hesitated before saying, "Yes."

After a little friendly conversation, I gave him the extra coupons from my flier along with a five-dollar bill. He thanked me profusely. Not looking left or right, he headed to the counter as I got up to leave.

> "One who is gracious to a poor man lends to the Lord, and He will repay him for his good deed" Proverbs 19:17, (NASB).

Another time I patronized my favorite hamburger and shake restaurant and bought a chocolate milkshake. I asked for a large styrofoam cup of ice water. By the time I had made it to the intersection three miles down the road, the milkshake was nearly consumed. My car waited in line for the red light to change, and a man with a homemade cardboard sign was sweltering in the hot noontime sun. With burned face and arms and sweat-drenched shirt, he approached me, having worked his way down the median.

I lowered the window and said, "I haven't a job to offer you, and I have no cash, but would you like this cup of cold water?" (I wished I hadn't just spent my last $2.98.)

He immediately replied, "Yes ma'am, thank you, thank you. God bless you." And the light turned green. In my rear view mirror, I saw the cup raised to his parched lips.

"And if anyone gives even a cup of cold water to one of these little ones because he is my disciple, I tell you the truth, he will certainly not lose his reward" (Matthew 10:42).

The young man acknowledged His Source before I could. Is there a chance he was a "disciple?" God had provided the cup, which I hadn't yet sipped from. It doesn't take much to give a blessing, but a reward is also promised to the giver.

Chapter Thirty-Six

Whatever outreach the church offers, the joy of giving to missions is like nothing else. Each February, my church hosts a missionary conference where missionaries returning from their assignments share how the Lord is at work through them. Sometimes the communication is skyped with those left behind, reconnecting us halfway around the world.

As a result of their stories, many in our congregation have decided to follow Jesus into fulltime work on the foreign field, or in jail ministry, or even to start sister churches. It's refreshing to observe fresh, innovative young Christians infused with Holy Spirit energy.

We also have a former pastor taking risks to plow new territory in Muslim countries, planting churches, and starting seminaries. Others serve where you cannot name their mission field. Helping support these missionaries requires a mammoth benevolence fund.

When I was a child, once a year, probably the only church call you'd receive was to collect pledges as the new budget was being planned. It's been many years since I belonged to a church that conducts every-member canvases. Rid of that practice, I've seen more faith exercised and more generous giving—not just giving to pay operating expenses. Of course, there are still many who haven't made the connection between just attending regularly and actually belonging to the family with its responsibilities and rewards.

One elder has played a major part in motivating members to pay down our church's mortgage—an example of excess giving so that the church could eliminate this debt five years early. Recently, a matching gift of $30,000 brought him to the front of the sanctuary. To thankful applause, he announced the goal had been met.

Lavish, sacrificial giving to bless the community where our church is located is another case in point. Our community work projects are an outreach to handle all sorts of handyman jobs — fix plumbing, replace leaky shingles, rake up yard trash, and much more. Our neighbors are served as brothers and sisters...believers/non believers, members/non members alike.

Afterwards, those who benefit from these fix-ups return with the workers to the church for lunch and fellowship. Rick Madsen, my son, has often been in charge of these workdays. His wife Wendy, with a hard-working crew, is in the church kitchen fixing many hearty lunches.

Over 125 projects have been completed through the years. I'm thankful to the crew for gifting me a workday. Much was accomplished that had burdened me so long. I was a very cheerful receiver.

Side by side with members, residents can participate in tending our community garden and egg-laying hens. Harvested vegetables and gathered eggs are distributed weekly to those in need by two of our members. Their personal visits bring cheer as good neighbors.

> "I will praise You, O Lord, with my whole heart; I will tell of all Your marvelous works. I will be glad and rejoice in You; I will sing praise to Your name, O Most High" Psalm 9:1-2, (NKJV).

Chapter Thirty-Seven

St. Paul's officers boldly plan the budget before they share it with the congregation; not afterwards to see how much money they have to work with. Asking for pledges or tithes is not our practice. Impractical? It's a matter of faith. Every gift, large or small is important, but leaning on the Holy Spirit's guidance is the secret. And then there's the unexpected—a natural catastrophe like a hurricane, and people respond generously.

During the 2017 storm season, we were dealt a heavy blow—Hurricane Irma flooded our sanctuary, blew over large trees and dealt major outside structural damage. The Women in the Church, WIC, delayed their fall brunch and turned it into a time of prayer and fasting with a special offering. Combined with the money saved by skipping food and decorations at the WIC event, over $2,000 went into the church's relief fund. As we have helped other churches in their crises in the past, we dug deeper for ourselves.

Our church sustained more damages than any other church nationwide in the Presbyterian Church of America (PCA) denomination. After inspection to assess damages, $60,000 poured in from Mission North America, the PCA relief fund, to help defray repairs. This amount equaled the high deductible on our property insurance. I thought of the Macedonian churches that the Apostle Paul praised for their cheerful giving to other churches in need. God had planned to dispatch His messengers before the need was even known.

II Corinthians 8:2-5 says, "Out of the most severe trial, their overflowing joy and their extreme poverty welled up in rich generosity. For I testify that they gave as much as they were able, and even beyond their ability. Entirely on their own" (NIV).

Our *Macedonian* benefactors are spread across the U.S.

In an Old Testament example of cheerful giving, the Israelites contributed to the construction of the tabernacle in response to Moses' instructions. Highly motivated, they were excessive in their generosity, and the craftsmen told Moses that more than enough had been received.

> "Then Moses gave an order and they sent this word throughout the camp: 'No man or woman is to make anything else as an offering for the sanctuary.' And so the people were restrained from bringing more, because what they already had was more than enough to do all the work" Exodus 36:6-7, (KJV).

God's people always have the wherewithal to meet the need if they only will.

Chapter Thirty-Eight

Today, in many churches, you can sign up to have a certain amount deducted from your bank account or charged to your credit card. Some larger churches have ATM machines in their foyers, or ushers stand by the exits with baskets. Watching a nearly empty offering plate pass by isn't so unusual under these circumstances. But it doesn't reflect the same attitude and practice of "bringing into His house tithes and offerings." It withholds from our children the visual lesson of obedience in giving, which they need to learn.

Personally, I want to put my gift into the offering plate as it's passed. It's a reminder that we are in community with fellow believers, and everything we have belongs to the Lord. Let's keep the giving of alms and offerings personal rather than technologically expedient.

Recently, the head usher in our church recruited two little boys to take up the offering. They appear to be eight and ten and, like the adult ushers, they adhere to rules of attendance and dress. Outfitted in suits, dress shirts and ties, their respectful behavior shows how seriously they have taken their training. Sometimes it's their turn to go before the altar as the offerings are dedicated to the Lord. Their sweet, innocent faces nearly move me to tears. This is a manifest lesson in "training up a child in the way he should go."

For a medium-sized congregation of around 400 regular attendees, we have a large budget. Weekly, the giving is reported year to date. Nearing the end of a difficult year we may lag behind, but the Lord hears our prayers. Meeting or exceeding the budget is the Lord's doing, and we rejoice cheerfully. "Bless the Lord, O my soul and all that is within me bless His holy name."

Chapter Thirty-Nine

Years ago I had a framed scripture which hung in my foyer: "Choose for yourselves this day whom you will serve. . . But as for me and my household, we will serve the Lord" Joshua 24:15, (RSV).

I want my legacy of cheerful giving to be handed down to family members and to each generation that follows. Ten of my grandchildren have been on mission trips. Their fund-raising letters have contained, in their own words, their purpose in sharing the Good News of Jesus Christ. As their grandmother, I have been proud to support them financially and prayerfully.

They've covered the four corners of the earth— Namibia, a medical mission on the Amazon River, South Africa, China, Mexico, Dominican Republic, and Uganda. My granddaughter, Laura, went on an 11-month, 11-country mission adventure with the

Great Race, beginning in South America, then Southeast Asia, and culminating in Africa. She safely survived the earthquake in Nepal. . . AFTER the colossal one in India where Laura and her teammates helped in rescue efforts. . . handing out bottles of water and blankets. The more difficult— digging through rubble for survivors, wrenched their hearts. The team never encountered a more severe mercy than was required on this mission.

Most of our family serve their Savior out of the overflow of their hearts. Granddaughters, Melody and Cody, and daughter, Barby, currently work in three different houses of worship. Endowed with musical abilities, others sing or play instruments in choruses or choirs. Jan, my eldest, took Christian service to a new level and married her pastor, Curt Heffelfinger, in March 2017. Now, I'm called "Mom" by a pastor. How blessed I am.

Chapter Forty

In September 2016, I was told that I had pancreatic cancer and I should get my things in order. The doctor who made the pronouncement, a stranger to me, was candidly unemotional as she shared the bad news.

My gastroenterologist who first detected something terribly wrong, advised against operating on the tumor. Age, being the first factor, the complexity of the Whipple Procedure, the second. Possible complications included death, and others undesirable I'd have to live with—the choice was wrought with hard issues.

The first consultation I had with a surgeon gave me appealing reasons to forgo an operation. He answered my daughter Barby's question, "If this were your decision to make for yourself, how would you choose."

Without hesitation, he responded, "I'd go fishing for three months."

"Maybe I'll go on a trip around the world for three months," I tried to make light of it.

I ultimately decided to fight for my life. I reasoned I'd simply head to my heavenly home later rather than sooner. Sometimes, I question if I made the right choice, for as Paul said, "To me to live is Christ, and to die is gain" Philippians 1:21, (NIV). A plaque over my desk reminds me daily.

So much to do, so little time. . . My husband's health carried the most weight. As his caregiver, *I should make what is best for him my deciding factor.* God opened the way for us to leave our 3/2 home in Oviedo and move to a one-bedroom, two-bath apartment at Westminster Winter Park. Such intricate timing—my children and Mitch's children facilitated preparations for the move to happen just two days before my surgery. I had only two weeks to review who to give my special treasures to. I wanted to make those choices before the possibility of my demise.

Yet, I entered into it with much glee. Really. Most of my belongings had a history behind them. Family made some of the selections, and so the "good stuff" — my grandmother's hand-painted china, sterling silver from my mother, crystal, and years of acquisitions and HI gifts — were chosen first. My oil paintings went to different family homes. Joy's paintings, for the most part, I kept, and their beauty dazzles our small apartment. Such a wonderful decision too, as they keep me remembering fond times with my old friend.

Most of the rest, like my furniture (lots of it), left on a truck, headed to thrift shop, which benefits hospice in Lake County. But all that was chosen by my heirs, now displayed in their homes, is a delight for me when I visit.

Knowing my closet space at Westminster would be more restricted than the lovely 8 x 9' dressing room we'd added to our home, I leafed through my clothes, and weeded out at least 50%. Most went to the Salvation Army, but the prettiest items I handpicked for friends I thought they'd look good on. I had two gorgeous dresses from Austria, one an evening outfit from Strasberg, and a dirndl from Vienna.

The second year we were married, Mitch insisted on buying me a red ultra suede three-piece outfit with Parisian details. Another of his extravagant gifts was a handmade jacket and matching purse chosen from an exhibitionist's tent at the Winter Park Art Festival. My collection of hats would not serve a purpose in my modified living status, so I hoped someone else with the same pleasure I had asserting my fashion style might wear them. Each of the 12 chapeau had their own story.

Not sure why, I couldn't part with my black faille evening gown from Lillie Rubin with the gold and silver "eyelash" embroidered sleeves. My sentimental attachment — that I wore it at my branch manager's promotion party, to my fifth wedding anniversary's dinner, and the night of the captain's dinner on the Alaskan cruise. I'll have at least one more gala celebration — the one at which this book is introduced. Then perhaps, the 44-year-old frock will be retired.

And then I fingered the lovely white silk St. John's suit given me under similar circumstances. My friend, Carolyn Gillean, invited me to her Maitland home a few months after her mother passed. She had saved from the estate sale certain nicer outfits with a view of offering them to friends. Though the suit was a size 12, and I most often wore two sizes smaller, I wanted it. I had it altered to fit, and it has hung in my closet for ten or more years. Why was I so eager to have it?

The answer has now become clear. You see, I always wear white to memorial services. Black does not denote the clear promise of resurrection as white does. To me white is clean, pure, and hopeful. In His economy, God has even planned the homecoming outfit I will wear — the white, silk St. John's suit. It has a lovely gold braid trim around the collarless neckline and bordering the cardigan style front.

My only additional adornment is the prized tiny *precious feet* pin, electroplated gold, of my sidewalk counseling days. One more case in point, God cares about little details, and not letting anything of value go to waste.

> "We are confident, I *say*, and willing rather to be absent from the body, and to be present with the Lord" II Corinthians 4:8, (KJV).

Chapter Forty-One

Of all the roles I've played in life, I have embraced motherhood as my greatest. I didn't play with dolls when I was a child, pretending to be a mother to small girlish toys, but as I reached puberty, my natural inclination was to be a wife and mother.

During my engagement, it wasn't so much a matter of how many children we were going to have, but how long to wait before getting pregnant and how much space between children. And yes, our perfect family would include a boy and a girl. I foolishly determined that I was going to be a better mother than mine, and we were not going to make the same mistakes my parents had made. The day came when I admitted to myself and my parents, they were the best. I exceeded more than my share of mistakes.

Like most couples today, we wanted to have a house of our own before our first child was born.

Our time frame was two years, and we accomplished that. Jan Leslie Madsen was born six weeks premature, but she was right on time. William Erick Madsen arrived 23 months later — that too, was as close to schedule as we intended. Was this our perfect family?

Then came our surprise. We were still practicing birth control, but whoops! I was pregnant in spite of it. Well, God had His own way, and I readily adapted to carrying this bundle from heaven, Barbara Kathleen Madsen. Secretly, I had always thought in terms of four children. So perhaps we were heading that way.

Turns out, Bill was satisfied with just two. He was coming round to three, but there would not be a fourth. When I knew just how strongly he felt about this, I prayed about having twins. In fact, we were in the planning stage of building our dream home. I was set on learning if my obstetrician thought I might have twins. *As if I could will them!* They couldn't yet detect the gender of the baby, but perhaps the doctor would hear two heartbeats. We'd choose the architect's rendering of a four-bedroom instead of a three-bedroom house.

We moved into our three-bedroom home when Barby was six-months old. And my bliss was totally complete. Of course, I had my hands full. I kept busy practically every minute of every day. I couldn't imagine how mothers held full-time jobs and maintained their responsibilities at home.

My children were fortunate to have both sets of grandparents living in town. They were doted on, but happily, without spoiling in the sense that many children are with tons of stuff. As they matured, material things mattered little. The older generation followed through on whatever disciplines we had in place. Both my in-laws and parents respected that. Today, my children would agree that I practiced a strict code of conduct, but they did not protest too much. They accepted the instructions of an amateur and thrived.

As previously mentioned, my three were two, five, and seven when my husband left. I began to experience being a so-called working mom by necessity. Women's libbers would now think I had more value as a woman, with *a real job*.

I considered how I could be home when my kids returned from school. Home Interiors & Gifts, Inc. allowed me to arrange my schedule to maximize time with my kids. My part-time job became a full-time career, eventually supporting six of us, making it possible for my children to pursue whatever education they wanted. They also learned the importance of pitching in toward the whole effort of making our family function.

As young adults, they all became independent and self-supporting. There never was a basement on my property where one could set up their own digs. It was understood that wouldn't have happened anyway. Twenty-six-year-old dependents weren't in my playbook. But that was a different era.

Fast forward to the present. My biological children have given me eleven grandchildren between them and six great-grandchildren. They lead very busy lives. They're active in their houses of worship, and serve the Lord with gladness.

"Train up a child in the way he should go and when he is old, he will not depart from it." I've appreciated how they've honored their mother (and their father while he was living).

When we learned that I had the most aggressive form of cancer, pancreatic, they shifted into high gear to help me survive this dreaded disease. From the outset, including the day of my diagnosis, my daughter-in-law, Wendy Madsen, took on responsibilities far beyond any mother-in-law's expectations.

It fell to Wendy, my driver, to give me the results of the endoscopic ultrasound when the anesthesia wore off.

My children and I consulted over the best option, and we chose life. We were hopeful the complicated Whipple Procedure would save me. Then the mighty four, Jan, Rick, Wendy, and Barby took over management of the operation, medical, hospital (which included 16 ER visits between Mitch and me in 2017), prescription drugs, doctor's appointments, oncology infusions, and hands-on care in our apartment. All this in addition to moving Mitch and me out of our home and into a one-bedroom apartment two days before surgery.

Included in my variety of episodes were pneumonia, dehydration, headaches, loss of speech, confusion, anemia, atrial fibrillation, breathlessness, chest pains, weight loss, hair loss, and exhaustion. I was too weak to fix my own breakfast, including pouring a bowl of dry cereal. Certainly, I was too weak to take care of my husband who had his own set of medical problems. My offspring, together with their spouses responded to calls any time, day or night.

The mighty four were present to also dispatch all Mitch's issues and hospitalizations with an uncommon grace and energy. They were always close for me to lean on when I couldn't walk straight and outfitted me with a health aid pendant to push for help if I fell when alone.

Jan resigned from her job as a vocational therapist. She was and is my go-to gal, drawing from her nurse's training. Barby switched days at her church's administrative duties. Rick and Wendy, who live just five blocks from me, were usually first to respond to emergencies and handling and replacement of the meds. Rick took over completing my income tax business with my CPA (what a drudge to put on a boy!) The mighty four set up morning duties which they shared, and my friend,

Kathleen Martin took the shifts on Saturday, and came immediately from the early morning service on Sundays.

As I lounged listlessly on the sofa watching them prepare my breakfast, I knew I was the most blessed mother/friend in the world. Barby, our social media diva, elicited prayers from many, many friends and other family members. Reading Facebook lifted my spirits, and gave me others to think about. Greeting cards kept streaming in the mail.

Their cheerful giving kept me trying, slugging away, when I felt I just wanted to chuck it all. Wendy handled the schedule, interfaced with doctors' offices and their assistants. All had several turns at taking me for my chemo-therapy which to my deepest gratitude, ended in August 2017. I finished editing my book, "Fascinating Women, Living by Faith" while receiving two units of blood.

Weeks after the chemo ended, most all the episodes, one by one, were never seen again. The cancer markers were greatly reduced and CT scans of the pancreas and again of the chest, mid-section and lower abdomen showed the area as clear. Gradually, I regained my strength, started driving again, went grocery shopping, and resumed going to church and Bible study.

Of all the experiences in life, this one has made me most grateful for my wonderful, cheerful, all-giving children, including my daughter-in-love.

Mitch's children gave of themselves to us. Son Mitch and his wife, Ashton came for a visit of a few days to spend time with his dad. Daughter, Nicole, made three trips to help her father in my absence, and Chris, Mitch's youngest, the only one living in the area, has spent many Saturdays with his dad. Their lunches out has boosted him when he's needed it most. There are few antidotes for depression and dementia.

I praise God for supplying all our needs according to His riches in glory. My heart has filled to the brim with joy to know that He is always with me.

My children's time and convenience has been sacrificed often to serve me, and I've never heard a complaint. These months have brought us all closer. I am cheered by their acts of kindness and love. Thank you, Lord, for having placed me in this atmosphere of dependency and helplessness where I have experienced the ultimate love and selflessness. Thank you for restoring my vigor and health even if it is only temporary. I leave myself in your care.

Chapter Forty-Two

To sum up, living a life of stewardship, I believe, incorporates more than just giving to church and outside ministries. It means not spending money where the corporate or small business is aligned with practices that are ungodly, such as the "violators" mentioned earlier. Businesses that take liberal positions in advertising on television, radio, or press are off limits to me. I won't spend my money on objectionable films — movies that are anti-Christian or obscene. I have the power to turn off or walk out.

All of these "rules" require diligence in ferreting out the offenders, but there are lists to be obtained for guidance with respect to airlines, banks, department stores, household products, and so forth.

No longer do I support the Boy Scouts or Girl Scouts, which began as Christian organizations.

Susan G. Komen gives to Planned Parenthood (don't they care that abortions cause breast cancer), so they will not receive from me. March of Dimes, in their quest to reduce birth defects, promotes amniocentesis shots, causing thousands of miscarriages yearly and also condones *therapeutic* abortions, which are not therapeutic to babies. Lastly, charities that pay their executives huge salaries do not receive from me.

May I digress at this juncture on the subject of stewardship. At last, I decided I had one more major gift in me. The "Gala Celebration" was my response of gratitude for living to finish book number three, "Fascinating Women, Living by Faith." Surviving cancer gave me another purpose--raise money for pancreatic cancer research. A whole new significance came into play. Presenting book number four, "Confessions of a Cheerful Giver," was my BIG SURPRISE as an additional fund raiser during the Gala Celebration at which it was announced. May raised funds help discover methods for earlier detection of this phantom disease. As 2017 ends, its hidden stealth claims the lives of nine out of ten found to have pancreatic cancer. PanCan.org is a great website to learn more.

Stewardship also determines who gets my vote in local or national elections. How money is spent, who reflects godly character and has a proven record of accountability. Anyone who is "pro-choice" is a non-starter in my book. Since socialists, and moderates of both parties compromise on issues that affect my Christian values, I vote conservatively.

I support our American flag, our National Anthem, our U. S. Constitution, and honor and respect our military forces. No matter who is elected President of the United States, Republican or Democrat, I am responsible to honor the office. The person who occupies the White House is my president. My duty is to work for a unified country, "one nation under God."

My bottom line is to follow the Bible in practice, and if there is a conflict between man's law and God's law. I fear God more. I'll risk everything to obey Him.

Matthew 25: 31-34, 31 tells is, "When the Son of man shall come in his glory, and all the holy angels with him, then shall he sit upon the throne of his glory: And before him shall be gathered all nations: and he shall separate them one from another, as a shepherd divideth his sheep from the goats: And he shall set the sheep on his right hand, but the goats on the left. Then shall the King say unto them on his right hand, 'Come, ye blessed of my Father, inherit the kingdom prepared for you from the foundation of the world,'" (KJV). Then follows the great litany of "hungry and you fed me, thirsty and you gave me drink, a stranger and you took me in, naked and you clothed me, sick and you visited me, in prison and you came to me."

Jesus promises, "Inasmuch as you have done it unto one of the least of these my brethren, ye have done it unto me" Matthew 25:40, (KJV).

I think back to Jerry Lewis and his clumsy falls and slapstick sparring against pretty boy Dean Martin over the female star in their films. However, Jerry's greatest contribution to mankind outshone Hollywood and revealed his true nature. He was a generous, kind, and thoughtful man—Jewish in background. I'd like to think he knew Jesus as savior.

Influenced by his instruction, "Give until it feels good," I have received the rewards of a cheerful giver. My journey to this place of joy and contentment was the road God laid for me–and I would not have changed a thing because every step of the way made me grow.

May my confessions inspire you to be more intentional, generous, creative, and cheerful in your giving and in your living. May you enjoy every step of your journey, too.

God bless you!

EPILOGUE

The contents of this small confessional were transferred from memory into my computer in less than three weeks. I believe the ease with which I wrote it affirms that the Spirit enabled me to share the foundation of my existence — I have been a cheerful giver.

Take hold of these principles and expect great things to happen. There are no words to express how grateful I have been for all my life. Both hard and sad times have yielded lessons that were not wasted. Would I want to do it over again? I don't want to live my life on the planet one minute longer than the Lord wants me here. Just as He has used me, His plan for you is amazing and unique. Don't let any opportunities slip away.

It has all been worth it. During my great adventures, including the chances I took and my seemingly hasty decisions, I believed God. "O taste and see that the Lord is good: blessed is the man that trusteth in him" Psalms 34:8, (KJV).

The occasion for introducing, "Confessions of a Cheerful Giver" is the Gala Celebration, planned for over a year. The date, February 10, 2018, a Saturday Matinee, is a gathering of hundreds of friends and family to mark:

1. The successful completion of the book, "Fascinating Women, Living by Faith," and to provide an opportunity to buy it and my other books of faith.

2. My life, saved from an aggressive cancer.

3. God's goodness and mighty power.

4. Appreciation for the women whose timeless stories will inspire others.

5. Thanksgiving for all who prayed and helped me defeat staggering odds.

6.   Lastly, committing the proceeds of this benefit to the Pancreatic Cancer Action Network whose goal is "to double pancreatic cancer survival by 2020 through private research and advocating for more federal research funding."

About the Author

May it be said of me when my time has come, "She lived a full life," - Judy Madsen Johnson.

I thought my season of writing books was over July of 2017 when my manuscript, "Fascinating Women, Living by Faith" was published. It had been in the making three years. Cancer held me back almost another year, and my determination strengthened to finish this work if it was the last thing I ever did.

"Joy Cometh in the Morning," my first biographical project, was taken on as a favor to Joy Postle Blackstone. From start to finish, it took from 1987 to

2011, 24 years—that may be a record, but not one to brag about. Finishing what I had begun had never been more critical to me. I had an outstanding subject, and feel I reproduced Joy as honestly and entertainingly as anyone could.

Grandma Moses sold her first painting when she was 76, and I sold my first book at 76.

As a wannabe artist, I chose "Writing with words on the landscape of life" for my tag line. I discovered how much I enjoyed using my computer to make brush strokes on fresh canvases—empty sheets of paper. Coloring in the details, using creative prose to fill in the blanks gave me a new found satisfaction.

In sequence, I had been a stay-at-home mother, a 21-year businesswoman selling home accessories, 20 years standing on the front lines in the war against abortion, and finally as an author since 2011, my fourth book has now been published.

Writing about what I know, I made the investment of time and effort to polish and refine my writing: Four writers' conferences, weekend retreats, eight years of monthly Word Weavers' critique groups, and four National League of American Pen Women Conferences.

I've just finished my fourth book, "Confessions of a Cheerful Giver," (over 21,000 words) three weeks after typing the first sentence. Perhaps there are a couple more books bouncing around inside I can "paint" in a few months.

I love sharing meaningful lives and events. It's become second nature to me now. At eighty-two, my mind is amazingly clear and focused — if this is God's purpose for me in my final years, I say "Bring it on."

CONTACT INFORMATION

Facebook Page: Judy Madsen Johnson

Website: judymadsenjohnson.com

Email Address: judymadsenjohnson@gmail.com

OTHER BOOKS BY THE AUTHOR

"Joy Cometh in the Morning, the Joy Postle Blackstone Story"

"Stories from the Front Lines, the Battle Against Abortion"

"Fascinating Women, Living by Faith"

Available through amazon.com

92894151R00109

Made in the USA
Columbia, SC
01 April 2018